CW01262870

Kate Bygrave © Copyright 2009

All Rights Reserved

No part of this publication may be reproduced, stored in a retrieval system, or transmitted in any form or by any means, electronic, mechanical, photocopying, recording or otherwise without prior permission of the copyright owner.

British Library Cataloguing In Publication Data
A Record of this Publication is available from the British Library

ISBN 978-1-4452-8407-1

Highest Echelons Publication

www.highestechelons.com

Email
ken.jackson@highestechelons.com

Words written on a page
My thoughts let out of their deepest cave
Emotions spilt across a line
Creativity nothing but all mine
My soul bare for all to read
And to you all I sincerely plead
Read this book with an open heart
As then hopefully I will share a part

Contents

Page 1	Gran Canaria
Page 2	Forbidden Fruit
Page 4	Relax/Music /The Magnetism Of Our Hearts
Page 5	Monogamous
Page 6	Playground Bully
Page 7	Time To Go Home/Ice Cream
Page 8	Women/Dad
Page 9	For My Mum
Page 10	Wishing Upon a Star/To Sense
Page 11	Ibiza
Page 12	We Are Blind
Page 13	Daddy
Page 16	Tear Drops
Page 17	My Mr. Pan/Thank You
Page 18	It's all about you
Page 19	Molly the Monster
Page 20	What am I?
Page 21	21st Century Cinderella
Page 22	BFF
Page 23	If I Carried You
Page 24	Simple Things You Do/Who could it be?
Page 25	Quick………Hide
Page 26	Losing You
Page 27	For my Sister
Page 28	Why Do We Worry?/I've Fallen
Page 29	Lost
Page 30	Char's Choc Brownies
Page 31	Standing Tall

Gran Canaria

Millions of miles and lands away
I'm lying on a beach or by the pool today
Sun is beaming on my pearly skin
I bet your wondering what I've done, where I've been
A plane has taken me to this destination
Myself and my best friend, Miss Michelle Mason
People bearing their bodies in full bloom
Nudist beaches in their boom
Alcohol oozing from our pores
Why did we say yes to those club rep tours
Two girls in their twenties from the land of booze
Tomorrow we bark on an all-day cruise
Something tells me its going to be sweet
A lot of new people we are destined to meet
After the sea is an exclusive foam rave
A place where no-one is expected to behave
A day of rest is sure to follow
No more drinking at that bar Apollo
As we are not run on Duracell
Our beds and sleep will do us well

Forbidden Fruit

You met at work
Friends at first
A longed glance across a room
A brisk touch as you pass
The stare of the eyes
The race of the heart
A magnet to the lips
One you never want to part
You let him in
Passion explored
A new love for your bed
Your heart and your head
Has fallen again
For this one is your life
The explosion of joy
You've found the one

But at home waits his wife
With his separate family life
If you knew
Your world would crash
Your heart would break
You've fallen for a big mistake

So shall I tell you
This news I've gained
Or do I leave you
To play his game
The decision is hard
Confusion is great
The hardest duty for being a mate

Relax

Sun setting on the island

Beauty washes over my soul

The tide gently rolls over the worn sand

Relaxation fills me with ecstasy from head to toe

Music

A beat different to that of my heart

Pumping different times apart

It enters my body and intrudes its way

To my brain on a mission to say

Use the beat and move your feet

Swing those hips and pout those lips

For the music is pulling at your strings

Manoeuvring your body to do magnificent things

The Magnetism Of Our Hearts

My heart attached to yours by a string

The bond we have is a symbolic thing

When miles apart it hurts us so

This fight against gravity like a yo-yo

Monogamous

Were we born to be monogamous
Or were we made to spread our wings
To be with one forever
We miss out on many things
To feel a different touch
To kiss a different kiss
To love a different love
Is this too much to miss
Do I need to spread my wings
Do I need to fly away
Is my love good to share
Is my love on its way
Or have I reached my destination
Where I have to stay

Playground Bully

You called me hurtful names
Used me in your nasty games
You made me hate my looks
I would hide behind my books
I'd walk down a different path
When I could hear your evil laugh
I'd pretend to be ill when mum caught me crying
Of course my mum knew I was lying
Why did you think you had the right
Just because I couldn't fight
Too shy to stand up to you
That whole year slowly flew
One day I couldn't take anymore
You'd left my confidence smashed on the floor
But out of nowhere I collected it up
This day you were out of luck
I turned around and threw back your nasty ways
Gone forever are your bullying days
Look at yourself and tell me what you see
I see nothing, and nothing can't bully me

Time To Go Home

Ready to leave a new world we found
Going back to spending the English pound
No more sun
No more sea
I wonder in which world I would rather be

Ice Cream

The blissful cool of your icy touch
The creamy richness I love so much
A piece of gold on a sunny day
No one can resist the charm full way
You slide so soft down the throat
Cools my body like a castle's moat
Oh what can you be?
An ice cream waiting just for me

Women

Every woman should feel beautiful within their own skin

You must love yourself before others can be let in

Breathe your own air

Enjoy your own space

Be whoever you want to be

Shining bright so the whole world can see

Dad

My love for you is growing strong

For you I am prepared to forgive all wrong

Half a life time has rolled on by

You missed it all in a blink of an eye

Hopefully we can gain some back

As the father daughter bond we do lack

Let's give it all we can

As dad I'd love to be your biggest fan

For My Mum

For you I share my deepest bond
You've guided me through life and beyond
Past events have made me strong
I don't regret the days you did wrong
As I too cared for you as well
When it happened, you deeply fell
Into the deepest of depression
I only have one tiny confession
Seeing you huddled in the corner
Shaking and crying, you felt like dying
A mask I put on to help you through
Inside I was dying as well as you
A moment a child should never see
I made sure the only child to see it was me
My sister protected from the damaging sight
I used all my love to make things right
But mum I don't begrudge you any of this
Although those moments I do not miss
You made it through to smile again
I love you my mum, my friend.

Wishing Upon a Star

I wished upon a star
For my dad who was afar
For a cookie from the jar

Then I wished upon a star
To be old enough to go to the bar
Or to drive my mum's car

Now I wish upon a star
For love and happiness, how bizarre

To Sense

To feel passion is an exploration of sensations
To eat passion is an explosion of senses

To be passion is an explicit way to sense
To have known passion is an expired sense of sensational senses

Ibiza

Laying on a desert sand
Light breeze does trickle across my hand
Sun beaming on my skin
Bird's happy song they sing

Head does pound
Like an awful sound
Eyes do ache
From last nights mistake
All the booze my pores do ooze
My bed I need
And grease to feed
This banging hangover
Release I plead

From the beach where I laid my head
I must find my hotel and crash in my bed
As tonight no doubt will be round two
What else in Ibiza are you meant to do?

We Are Blind

Is their peace in the world
Or are we blind
To a monster unleashing
On the other side
The guns and the knives
The hurt and the pain
The lives that are lost
Due to someone's gain
Families lost
Friends are gone
People lay starving
Their lives are none
Is your life really that bad
Would you swap with those who suffer
Abused all day to afford their supper
I somehow don't think so
And neither would I
But think how you can help
Before more innocent die

Daddy

My memories of you
Are small and vague
As when you left us
Our lives were plagued
Banished us from your life
Left us with no home
My sister's tiny eyes
All lost and confused
Why has daddy left us alone
Mummy all battered and bruised
Did you love us then
Do you love us now
For that is a daddy
I cannot be proud

Years go past
No contact
No call
Our lives grew empty
Of no father at all
Was it my fault you kicked us out

Did I not tidy my toys
Did I scream and shout
Was I naughty
Was I boring
Was it me you hated
Or was this whole thing fated

Years have passed
We have grown
Stories we learnt from families and friends
You were the devil
Could you ever make amends

More years have gone
The telephone rings
Life can throw you
The most absent of things
My dad has called
The stranger on the phone
A voice I don't recognise
Is it my own
My dad I had lost

And now have found
He wants to reconcile
The time that's past
Can I forgive him the last
Eighteen odd years I have had no father
My head says no
But my heart would rather
Love and see and hold him tight
Squeeze him close with all my might
But did you love us then
Do you love us now
Are you here to stay
Or exit with a bow
For my life is not a play
You are either here to stay
Or forgiveness I can not grant you

Then a bomb falls out the sky
It hits me and I start to cry
Cancer you say
Is eating your body

My heart it crashes
My head confused
My life's in a whirlwind
My face bemused

How can I not forgive his past
Is this opportunity going to be my last
To know my father and let him in
As cancer is a battle we do not always win

Tear Drop

Not a tear drop from my eye
Not a rain drop from the sky
But the whole world's trying to cry on me

Is it time to say goodbye
Was a dove born to fly?
Can the answer be denied from me?

My Mr. Pan

The highest mountain
The furthest sea
How far would you travel to rescue me
I was stolen onto a pirate ship
By a smelly pirate called shark fin tip
Would you risk your life for one last kiss
For when our lips touch it is loves true bliss
Are you my Peter Pan, will you fight this hook
Or do the happy endings only happen in the story book

Thank You

You took me in when I needed a home
Looked after me as I've grown
You both share a glowing halo
You live in the sticks, that's ok though
Games we played, we looked so crazy
The crash and the icy days are kind of hazy
So much love you have to give
I'm glad I was there for you to share it with
To my beautiful god parents, thanks for having me
To have you around I can live happily

It's all about you

It's all about you
From when our eyes locked eyes
I knew you were the one
The shape of your face
The stance of your body
The outfit you wore
The courage I saw

It's all about you
From when our lips locked lips
I knew you were the one
The touch of your skin
The feel of your hands
The passion in the hold
The grasp so bold

It's all about you
From when our hearts locked hearts
I knew you were the one
You are the one

Molly the Monster

Hidden quietly in a corner
A foot walks past the entrance to her cave
Out she bursts in an excited rage
The foot someone will have to save
She bites and chews on the helpless prey
A cute little kitten you can longer say
The growth to a cat is on its way
But forever Molly monster will want to play
Presents she leaves by the back door
A leaf, a frog or a rabbits paw
Sits there proud and full of glee
The presents we don't receive so happily
Maybe if she bought us a money tree
But for Molly monster the best present must be
Living with a kind and loving family

What am I?

Some days I travel the world
Some days I only reach the end of the street
It all depends on the way you lift me
If you set me free
What am I?
I am the pollen from the flower and the tree
I am the dust floating endlessly
From me to you
From you to me
Travel by wind or bee
I am not exclusive
I do not decide my fate
Whether I land on you
Or another
You'll never be my soul mate

21st Century Cinderella

As I fell from the height of my heel
My strong shining knight did kneel
Saved me from falling to the ground
The sight of him made my heart pound
The spark between us ignited
Our lips were fully excited
As leaning in for a kiss
It's one I'll truly miss
As my phone sang
The taxi had rang
One more second he'll wait
Goodbye my knight, If we shall meet again
We'll have to leave that to fate

BFF

You are always there
You will always care
Relationship, family or work trouble
You are always there
To burst my tear filled bubble
Happy, stressed or upset
You will always care
That my emotional needs are met
You are my best friend
You share my pain
I share your pain
And we never give each other pain
From each other we can only gain
You my friend I will always love
Until the days we reach high above

If I Carried You

If I carried you across a river
Would you sail me home
Or would you leave me there
To swim back all alone

If I carried you across a dessert
Would you fly me home
Or would you leave me there
To crawl back all alone

If I gave you my hand to hold
Would you give me your heart and soul
Or would you leave me out in the cold
To face this world alone

Simple Things You Do

Explosion of Joy
Eyes fill with tears
Smile wipes across my face
Body rushes with excitement
Heart beats fast
What has happened?
You have smiled at me

Who could it be?

Male attention is at its high
But I am not interested, why oh why
No I have not just fallen from the lemon tree
There is only one guy with whom I would rather be

Quick.........Hide

Bang bang bang on the front door
Bodies lay out on the living room floor
He wants to get in
He wants to cause harm
Is he going to grab by the throat or the arm
Quick someone call 999
Will he get arrested or just another fine
Close the windows lock the doors
Forced to act like animals on all fours
Hide from sight, hide from view
Who's he after, me or you
All goes quiet, not a sound
Has he snuck in, has he found his way round
Lot's of fears we prepare for a fight
He tries to get in with all his might
On my birthday my friends witness his rage
Like a wild beast let loose from its cage
Police arrive, all is done
Well done girls, this time we've won

Losing You

When people die,
A hole is left in the world
Hearts are broken
Tears fall
Depression sets in
When do these negative energies heal?
Do they ever fully heal?
Can you live life as you once did before?
Or does death linger over you like a cloud throughout
your whole existence?
Is it easier not to love, so we feel no pain?
Or do we feel more pain through lack of love?
Does new love for another, heal that of a lost love?
Can time heal pain?
When people we love die
Do we die ourselves?

For my Sister

We've been through times of the deepest sad
Many of which were because of our dad
But through the bad times
Came a stronger bond
For you my sister I am very fond
When I am low, you bring the glow
My love for you will always grow
Your funny, dippy and crazy ways
Are forever moments, not just a phase
My blood is your blood
My name is your name
My nose is your nose
But that's all that's the same
You'll always be deep in my heart
No matter the distance between us
We will never part

Why Do We Worry?

The tiniest things can make us stress
Can put your life in such a whirlwind mess
Make things worse than they really are
Make a good thing once close, now afar
Chill a minute and take a step back
Chuck those worries in the dustbin sack
Free that smile and fight those fears
A beauty like yours should shed no tears

I've Fallen

The night I met you
I caught your eye
The night I kissed you
I caught your heart
Maybe not love at first sight
But love at first kiss we could not fight
Looking into your eyes
It lifts me to the furthest skies
With you I am on cloud nine
Without you I am watching time

Lost

What am I feeling

Lost, confused and strayed

Why am I feeling this way

I don't know, that is why I am confused

My life isn't that bad

Is it just one of those days

Or is depression on its way

Please save me this day

Tomorrow will be better

Just to get through the day

That is all I need

Wake up afresh

With a smile

With a breeze

Surely the lost confused and strayed me

Will be lost forever

Char's Choc Brownies

Feed me sweetness

To fuel my soul

Sugar flows through my veins

Straight from the chocolate bowl

Is it greed

Or is it must

Or is it my taste buds

Full with lust

For my lips it touches

And then my tongue

My brains sensation

Is then rung

No matter for

Must, greed or lust

This temptation

Is one I trust

Standing Tall

Through the distance and time
I spend on my own
I fight the fears of being alone
It's time to enjoy being
With me, myself and I
To hold the tears
When I start to cry
Be Independent
Be strong
As then it won't be long
Till your heart is found
With feet on the ground
You find yourself
And you can now be found.

Printed in Great Britain by
Amazon.co.uk, Ltd.,
Marston Gate.